Zilpha Harlow Spooner

Poems of the Pilgrims

Zilpha Harlow Spooner

Poems of the Pilgrims

ISBN/EAN: 9783337293802

Printed in Europe, USA, Canada, Australia, Japan

Cover: Foto ©Thomas Meinert / pixelio.de

More available books at **www.hansebooks.com**

POEMS OF THE PILGRIMS

SELECTED BY

ZILPHA H. SPOONER

"That little Mayflower, convoyed by the winds
And the rude waters to our rocky shore,
Shall scatter Freedom's seed throughout the world;
And all the nations of the earth shall come
Singing to share the harvest-home of Truth."
                                          LOWELL

BOSTON
A. WILLIAMS AND COMPANY
283 WASHINGTON STREET
1882

To

JOSEPH HENRY STICKNEY, Esq.

OF BALTIMORE, MD.

WHOSE HEARTFELT INTEREST IN ALL THAT RELATES TO THE PILGRIMS,

AND WHOSE MUNIFICENT GIFTS

TO REBUILD, BEAUTIFY, AND PRESERVE PILGRIM HALL,

ENTITLE HIM TO THE HIGH REGARD OF

ALL WHO REVERENCE THE FOUNDERS OF OUR COUNTRY,

This Volume

IS RESPECTFULLY DEDICATED

BY

THE COMPILER.

CONTENTS.

		PAGE
ROBINSON OF LEYDEN	O. W. Holmes	7
THE EMBARKATION	Lizzie Doten	10
SONG OF THE PILGRIMS	T. C. Upham	15
THE PILGRIMS	Mrs. Sigourney	17
HYMN	William Cullen Bryant	21
THE LIBERTY SONG	John Dickinson	22
NEW ENGLAND	J. G. Percival	25
SONG	Alexander Scammel	28
HYMN. A ROCK IN THE WILDERNESS	Anonymous	30
ODE FOR DECEMBER 22, 1792	John Davis	31
MEMORY OF OUR FATHERS	Flint	34
HYMN. DECEMBER 22, 1799	Samuel Davis	35
THE PILGRIM FATHERS	Charles Sprague	37
HYMN. DECEMBER 22, 1803	John Quincy Adams	42
ODE	Rufus Dawes	44
CLARK'S ISLAND	Hersey B. Goodwin	47
HYMN	Leonard Bacon	49
ODE	Samuel Davis	50
HYMN. DECEMBER 22, 1806	Rev. Dr. Holmes	52
FOREFATHERS' DAY, DECEMBER 22	M. W. Chapman	54
SONG. DECEMBER 22, 1807	Joseph Warren Brackett	56
THE PILGRIM'S VISION	O. W. Holmes	61
HYMN	George Russell	67

CONTENTS.

	PAGE
THE LANDING OF THE PILGRIM FATHERS IN NEW ENGLAND............Mrs. Hemans	69
THE PILGRIM FATHERS............Ebenezer Elliott	72
TWO HUNDRED YEARS AGO............James Flint	74
HYMN. SUNG AT THE CELEBRATION, DECEMBER 22, 1824............William P. Lunt	78
ODE............Grenville Mellen	81
HYMN. DECEMBER 22, 1831............Anonymous	85
NATIONAL HYMN............David Lee Child	87
REMEMBRANCE OF THE PILGRIMS............Anonymous	89
HYMN............S. Deane	91
THE SAINTED SIRES............Anonymous	93
ODE............John Pierpont	95
HYMN FOR DECEMBER 22, 1870............Nathaniel Spooner	97
STANZAS FROM "THE PRESENT CRISIS"............J. R. Lowell	98

INDEX OF FIRST LINES.

	PAGE
ALL hail the day that ushers in	28
A rock in the wilderness welcomed our sires	30
A voice of grief and anger	72
Come, join hand and hand, brave Americans all	22
Come listen to my story	74
God hath from age to age	87
Great God of all! in humble, grateful prayer	97
Hail, hallowed spot! where Freedom's rays	47
Hail, Pilgrim Fathers of our race	35
Hail, sons of the Pilgrims, assembled to pay	56
Hail to the land whereon we tread,	25
He sleeps not here; in hope and prayer	7
Holy spot! where glowing choirs	78
How slow yon tiny vessel ploughs the main!	17
In pleasant lands have fallen the lines	34
In the hour of twilight shadows	61
Let children learn the mighty deeds	50
Lo, the rising star of Freedom	91
Not all the loftiest memories	81
O God, beneath thy guiding hand	49
Our fathers' God! to Thee we raise	52
Sons of New England sires	44
Sons of renowned sires	31
Sons of the noble sires	67

	PAGE
The band of Pilgrim exiles in tearful silence stood	10
The breaking waves dashed high	69
The breeze has swelled the whitening sail	15
The brittle bark is on the gale	85
The memory of the faithful dead	54
The Pilgrim Fathers, — where are they?	95
They come, — that coming who shall tell?	37
'T is as easy to be heroes as to sit the idle slaves	98
When o'er the billows heaving deep	42
While Pilgrims' sons, a festive throng	93
Wild was the day, the wintry sea	21
With joy I heard them say	89

POEMS OF THE PILGRIMS.

ROBINSON OF LEYDEN.

HE sleeps not here; in hope and prayer
    His wandering flock had gone before,
But he, the shepherd, might not share
    Their sorrows on the wintry shore.

Before the Speedwell's anchor swung,
    Ere yet the Mayflower's sail was spread,
While round his feet the Pilgrims clung,
    The pastor spake, and thus he said:

"Men, brethren, sisters, children dear!
    God calls you hence from over sea;
Ye may not build by Haerlem Meer,
    Nor yet along the Zuyder-Zee.

"Ye go to bear the saving word
    To tribes unnamed and shores untrod:

Heed well the lessons ye have heard
   From those old teachers taught of God.

"Yet think not unto them was lent
   All light for all the coming days,
And Heaven's eternal wisdom spent
   In making straight the ancient ways.

"The living fountain overflows
   For every flock, for every lamb,
Nor heeds, though angry creeds oppose
   With Luther's dike or Calvin's dam."

He spake; with lingering, long embrace,
   With tears of love and partings fond,
They floated down the creeping Maas,
   Along the isle of Ysselmond.

They passed the frowning towers of Briel,
   The "Hook of Holland's" shelf of sand,
And grated soon with lifting keel
   The sullen shores of Fatherland.

No home for these! too well they knew
   The mitred king behind the throne;
The sails were set, the pennons flew,
   And westward ho! for worlds unknown.

And these were they who gave us birth,
    The Pilgrims of the sunset wave,
Who won for us this virgin earth,
    And freedom with the soil they gave.

The pastor slumbers by the Rhine, —
    In alien earth the exiles lie. —
Their nameless graves our holiest shrine,
    His words our noblest battle-cry!

Still cry them, and the world shall hear,
    Ye dwellers by the storm-swept sea!
Ye *have* not built by Haerlem Meer,
    Nor on the land-locked Zuyder-Zee!
O. W. HOLMES.

THE EMBARKATION.

"So they left that goodly and pleasant city, which had been their resting-place near twelve years. But they knew they were *pilgrims* and looked not much to those things; but lifted their eyes to heaven, their dearest country, and quieted their spirits." — E. WINSLOW.

The band of Pilgrim exiles in tearful silence stood,
While thus outspake, in parting, John Robinson the good:
"Fare thee well, my brave Miles Standish! thou hast a trusty sword;
But not with carnal weapons shalt thou glorify the Lord.
Fare thee well, good Elder Brewster! thou art a man of prayer;
Commend the flock I give thee to the Holy Shepherd's care.
And thou, belovéd Carver, — what shall I say to thee?
I have need, in this my sorrow, that thou shouldst comfort me.

In the furnace of affliction must all be sharply
 tried ;
But naught prevails against us, if the Lord be on
 our side.
Farewell, farewell, my people! go, and stay not
 the hand,
But precious seed of Freedom sow ye broadcast
 through the land.
Ye may scatter it in sorrow, and water it with
 tears,
But rejoice for those who gather the fruit in after
 years ;
Ay! rejoice that ye may leave them an altar unto
 God,
On the holy soil of Freedom, where no tyrant's
 foot hath trod.
All honor to our sovereign, his majesty King
 James,
But the King of kings above us the highest hom-
 age claims."
Upon the deck together they knelt them down and
 prayed, —
The husband and the father, the matron and the
 maid ;
The broad blue heavens above them, bright with
 the summer's glow,

And the wide, wide waste of waters, with its treacherous waves below;
Around, the loved and cherished, whom they should see no more,
And the dark, uncertain future stretching dimly on before.
Oh, well might Edward Winslow look sadly on his bride!
Oh, well might fair Rose Standish press to her chieftain's side!
For with crucified affections they bowed the knee in prayer,
And besought that God would aid them to suffer and to bear;
To bear the cross of sorrow — a broader shield of love
Than the Royal Cross of England, that proudly waved above.
The balmy winds of summer swept o'er the glittering seas;
It brought the sign of parting, — the white sails met the breeze;
One farewell gush of sorrow, one prayerful blessing more,
And the bark that bore the exiles glided slowly from the shore.

THE EMBARKATION. 13

"Thus they left that goodly city," o'er stormy seas
    to roam;
"But they knew that they were pilgrims," and
    this world was not their home.

There is a God in heaven, whose purpose none
    may tell;
There is a God in heaven, who doeth all things
    well:
And thus an infant nation was cradled on the deep,
While hosts of holy angels were set to guard its
    sleep;
No seer, no priest, or prophet, read its horoscope
    at birth,
No bard in solemn saga sung its destiny to earth;
But slowly, slowly, slowly as the acorn from the
    sod,.
It grew in strength and grandeur, and spread its
    arms abroad.
The eyes of distant nations turned towards that
    goodly tree,
And they saw how fair and pleasant were the
    fruits of Liberty!
Like earth's convulsive motion before the earth-
    quake's shock,

Like the foaming of the ocean around old Plymouth Rock,
So the deathless love of Freedom, the majesty of Right,
In all kindred and all nations, is rising in its might ;
And words of solemn warning come from the honored dead, —
" Woe, woe to the oppressor if righteous blood be shed !
Rush not blindly on the future ! Heed the lessons of the past !
For the feeble and the faithful are the conquerors at last."

Lizzie Doten.

SONG OF THE PILGRIMS.

The breeze has swelled the whitening sail,
The blue waves curl beneath the gale,
And, bounding with the wave and wind,
We leave Old England's shores behind.
 Leave behind our native shore,
 Homes, and all we loved before.

The deep may dash, the winds may blow,
The storm spread out its wings of woe
Till sailors' eyes can see a shroud
Hung in the folds of every cloud;
 Still, as long as life shall last,
 From that shore we 'll speed us fast.

For we would rather never be
Than dwell where mind cannot be free,
But bows beneath a despot's rod
Even where it seeks to worship God.
 Blasts of heaven, onward sweep!
 Bear us o'er the troubled deep!

Oh, see what wonders meet our eyes!
Another land and other skies!
Columbian hills have met our view!
Adieu! Old England's shores, adieu!
    Here, at length, our feet shall rest,
    Hearts be free, and homes be blessed.

As long as yonder firs shall spread
Their green arms o'er the mountain's head, —
As long as yonder cliffs shall stand,
Where join the ocean and the land, —
    Shall those cliffs and mountains be
    Proud retreats for liberty.

Now to the King of kings we'll raise
The pean loud of sacred praise;
More loud than sounds the swelling breeze,
More loud than speak the rolling seas!
    Happier lands have met our view!
    England's shores, adieu! adieu!

T. C. UPHAM.

THE PILGRIMS.

How slow yon tiny vessel ploughs the main!
Amid the heavy billows now she seems
A toiling atom, — then from wave to wave
Leaps madly, by the tempest lashed, — or reels,
Half wrecked, through gulfs profound.
                              Moons wax and wane,
But still that lonely traveler treads the deep.
I see an ice-bound coast, toward which she steers
With such a tardy movement that it seems
Stern Winter's hand hath turned her keel to stone,
And sealed his victory on her slippery shrouds.
They land! They land! — not like the Genoese,
With glittering sword, and gaudy train, and eye
Kindling with golden fancies. — Forth they come
From their long prison, — hardy forms, that brave
The world's unkindness, — men of hoary hair,
And virgins of firm heart, and matrons grave,
Who hush the wailing infant with a glance.
Bleak Nature's desolation wraps them round, —
Eternal forests, and unyielding earth,

And savage men, who through the thickets peer
With vengeful arrow.   What could lure their
        steps
To this drear desert?   Ask of him who left
His father's home to roam through Haran's wilds,
Distrusting not the Guide who called him forth,
Nor doubting, though a stranger, that his seed
Should be as Ocean's sands.
                      But yon lone bark
Hath spread her parting sail.
                      They crowd the strand,
Those few, lone pilgrims.   Can ye scan the woe
That wrings their bosoms, as the last frail link
Binding to man and habitable earth
Is severed?   Can ye tell what pangs were there,
What keen regrets, what sickness of the heart,
What yearnings o'er their forfeit land of birth,
Their distant dear ones?
                      Long with straining eye
They watch the lessening speck.   Heard ye no
        shriek
Of anguish, when that bitter loneliness
Sank down into their bosoms?   No! they turn
Back to their dreary, famished huts, and pray!—
Pray,— and the ills that haunt this transient life
Fade into air.   Up in each girded breast

There sprang a rooted and mysterious strength, —
A loftiness, — to face a world in arms, —
To strip the pomp from sceptres, — and to lay
Upon the sacred altar the warm blood
Of slain affections, when they rise between
The soul and God.
     And can ye deem it strange
That from *their* planting such a branch should
  bloom
As nations envy? Would a germ, embalmed
With prayer's pure tear-drops, strike no deeper
  root.
Than that which mad ambition's hand doth strew
Upon the winds, to reap the winds again?
Hid by its veil of waters from the hand
Of greedy Europe, their bold vine spread forth
In giant strength.
     Its early clusters, crushed
In England's wine-press, gave the tyrant host
A draught of deadly wine. O ye who boast
In your free veins the blood of sires like these,
Lose not their lineaments. Should Mammon cling
Too close around your heart, or wealth beget
That bloated luxury which eats the core
From manly virtue, or the tempting world

Make faint the Christian purpose in your soul,
Turn ye to Plymouth's beach, — and on that rock
Kneel in *their* foot-prints, and renew the vow
They breathed to God.
Mrs. Sigourney.

HYMN.

Wild was the day; the wintry sea
   Moaned sadly on New England's strand,
When first, the thoughtful and the free,
   Our fathers, trod the desert land.

They little thought how pure a light,
   With years, should gather round that day;
How love should keep their memories bright,
   How wide a realm their sons should sway.

Green are their bays; and greener still
   Shall round their spreading fame be wreathed,
And regions now untrod shall thrill
   With reverence, when their names are breathed.

Till where the sun, with softer fires,
   Looks on the vast Pacific's sleep,
The children of the Pilgrim sires
   This hallowed day like us shall keep.

                William Cullen Bryant.

THE LIBERTY SONG.

SUNG AT THE FIRST CELEBRATION OF THE LANDING OF THE FOREFATHERS AT PLYMOUTH, DECEMBER 22, 1769.

Come, join hand and hand, brave Americans all,
And rouse your bold hearts at fair Liberty's call;
No tyrannous acts shall suppress your just claim,
Or stain with dishonor America's name.

CHORUS.

In Freedom we're born, and in Freedom we'll live;
   Our purses are ready,
   Steady, friends, steady,
Not as Slaves, but as Freemen, our money we'll give.

Our worthy Forefathers — let's give 'em a cheer —
To climates unknown did courageously steer;
Through oceans to deserts for freedom they came,
And dying, bequeathed us their freedom and fame.

Their generous bosoms all danger despised,
So highly, so wisely, their birthright they prized;

We'll keep what they gave, — we will piously keep,
Nor frustrate their toils on the land or the deep.

The Tree their own hands had to Liberty reared
They lived to behold growing strong and revered;
With transport they cried, " Now our wishes we gain,
For our children shall gather the fruits of our pain."

How sweet are the labors that Freemen endure,
That they shall enjoy all the profits secure.
No more such sweet labors Americans know
If Britons shall reap what Americans sow.

Swarms of placemen and pensioners soon will appear,
Like locusts deforming the charms of the year;
Suns vainly will rise, showers vainly descend,
If we are to drudge for what others shall spend.

Then join hand in hand, brave Americans all; .
By uniting we stand, by dividing, we fall;
In so righteous a cause let us hope to succeed,
For Heaven approves of each generous deed.

All ages shall speak with amaze and applause
Of the courage we 'll show in support of our laws;
To *die* we can *bear*, but to *serve* we *disdain;*
For *shame* is to *Freemen* more dreadful than *pain*.

This bumper I crown for our Sovereign's health,
And this for Britannia's glory and wealth;
That wealth and that glory immortal may be
If she is but *just* and we are but *free*.

JOHN DICKINSON.

NEW ENGLAND.

Hail to the land whereon we tread,
    Our fondest boast;
The sepulchre of mighty dead,
The truest hearts that ever bled,
Who sleep on Glory's brightest bed,
    A fearless host;
No slave is here — our unchained feet
Walk freely, as the waves that beat
    Our coast.

Our fathers crossed the ocean's wave
    To seek this shore;
They left behind the coward slave
To welter in his living grave; —
With hearts unbent, and spirits brave,
    They sternly bore
Such toils as meaner souls had quelled;
But souls like these such toils impelled
    To soar.

Hail to the morn, when first they stood
    On Bunker's height,
And, fearless, stemmed the invading flood,
And wrote our dearest rights in blood,
And mowed in ranks the hireling brood,
    In desperate fight!
Oh, 'twas a proud, exulting day,
For even our fallen fortunes lay
    In light.

There is no other land like thee,
    No dearer shore;
Thou art the shelter of the free;
The home, the port of Liberty,
Thou hast been, and shalt ever be,
    Till time is o'er.
Ere I forget to think upon
My land, shall mother curse the son
    She bore.

Thou art the firm, unshaken rock,
    On which we rest;
And, rising from thy hardy stock,
Thy sons the tyrant's frown shall mock,
And Slavery's galling chains unlock,
    And free the oppressed:

All who the wreath of Freedom twine
Beneath the shadow of their vine
    Are blest.

We love thy rude and rocky shore,
    And here we stand:
Let foreign navies hasten o'er,
And on our heads their fury pour,
And peal their cannons' loudest roar,
    And storm our land;
They still shall find our lives are given
To die for home, — and leant on Heaven
    Our hand.
J. G. Percival.

SONG.

DECEMBER 22, 1770.

ALL hail the day that ushers in
The period of revolving time,
In which our sires of glorious fame
Bravely through toils and dangers came

Novanglia's wilds to civilize,
And wild disorder harmonize;
To plant Britannia's arts and arms,
Plenty, peace, freedom, pleasing charms,

Derived from British rights and laws,
That justly merit our applause.
Darlings of Heaven, heroes brave,
You still shall live though in the grave.

Live, live, within each grateful breast,
With reverence for your names possessed;
Your praises on our tongues shall dwell,
And sires to sons your actions tell.

SONG.

To distant poles their praise resound,
Let virtue be with glory crowned;
Ye dreary wilds, each rock and cave,
Echo the virtues of the brave.

They nobly braved their indigence,
Death, famine, sword, and pestilence;
Each toil, each danger they endured,
Till for their sons they had procured

A fertile soil, profusely blest
With Nature's stores, and now possessed
By sons who gratefully revere
Our Fathers' names and memories dear.

Plymouth the great Mausoleum,
Famous for our Forefathers' Tomb,
Join, join the chorus, one and all,
Resound their deeds in Colony Hall.

ALEXANDER SCAMMEL.

HYMN.

A ROCK IN THE WILDERNESS.

A ROCK in the wilderness welcomed our sires
   From bondage far over the dark rolling sea;
On that holy altar they kindled the fires,
   Jehovah, which glow in our bosoms for thee.

Thy blessings descended in sunshine and shower,
   Or rose from the soil that was sown by thy hand;
The mountain and valley rejoiced in thy power,
   And heaven encircled and smiled on the land.

The Pilgrims of old an example have given
   Of mild resignation, devotion, and love,
Which beams like the star in the blue vault of heaven, —
A beacon-light hung in the mansions above.

In church and cathedral we kneel in our prayer,
   Their temple and chapel were valley and hill;
But God is the same in the aisle or the air,
   And He is the Rock that we lean upon still.

                       ANONYMOUS.

ODE.

WRITTEN FOR THE CELEBRATION, DECEMBER 22, 1792.

    Sons of renowned sires,
    Join in harmonious choirs,
        Swell your loud songs;
    Daughters of peerless dames
    Come with your mild acclaims,
    Let their revered names
        Dwell on your tongues.

    From frowning Albion's seat
    See the famed band retreat,
        On ocean tost;
    Blue tumbling billows roar,
    By keel scarce ploughed before,
    And bear them to this shore
        Fettered with frost.

    By yon wave-beaten rock
    See the illustrious flock
        Collected stand;

To seek some sheltering grove
Their faithful partners move,
Dear pledges of their love
    In either hand.

Not winter's sullen face,
Not the fierce tawny race
    In arms arrayed, —
Not hunger shook their faith,
Not sickness' baleful breath,
Nor Carver's early death,
    Their souls dismayed.

Watered by heavenly dew,
The germ of Empire grew, —
    Freedom its root;
From the cold northern pine,
Far t'ward the burning line,
Spreads the luxuriant vine
    Bending with fruit.

Columbia, child of Heaven!
The best of blessings given
    Be thine to greet;
Hailing this votive day,

ODE.

Looking with fond survey
Upon the weary way
    Of Pilgrim feet.

Here trace the moss-grown stones
Where rest their mouldering bones,
    Again to rise;
And let thy sons be led
To emulate the dead,
While o'er their tombs they tread
    With moistened eyes.

Sons of renowned sires,
Join in harmonious choirs,
    Swell your loud songs;
Daughters of peerless dames
Come with your mild acclaims,
Let their revered names
    Dwell on your tongues.

                JOHN DAVIS.

MEMORY OF OUR FATHERS.

In pleasant lands have fallen the lines
   That bound our goodly heritage,
And safe beneath our sheltering vines
   Our youth is blest, and soothed our age.

What thanks, O God, to Thee are due,
   That Thou didst plant our fathers here;
And watch and guard them as they grew,
   A vineyard to the planter dear.

The toils they bore our ease have wrought;
   They sowed in tears — in joy we reap;
The birthright they so dearly bought
   We'll guard, till we with them shall sleep.

Thy kindness to our fathers shown,
   In weal and woe through all the past,
Their grateful sons, O God, shall own,
   While here their name and race shall last.
FLINT.

HYMN.

DECEMBER 22, 1799.

Hail, Pilgrim Fathers of our race!
With grateful hearts your toils we trace;
Again this votive day returns,
And finds us bending o'er your urns.

Jehovah's arm prepared the road;
The heathen vanished at his nod;
He gave his vine a lasting root;
He loads its goodly boughs with fruit.

The hills are covered with its shade;
Its thousand shoots like cedars spread;
Its branches to the sea expand,
And reach to broad Superior's strand.

Of peace and truth the gladsome ray
Smiles in our skies and cheers the day;
And a new Empire's splendent wheels
Roll o'er the top of Western hills.

Hail, Pilgrim Fathers of our race!
With grateful hearts your toils we trace;
Oft as this votive day returns
We'll pay due honors to your urns.

SAMUEL DAVIS.

THE PILGRIM FATHERS.

They come — that coming who shall tell?
The eye may weep, the heart may swell,
But the poor tongue in vain essays
A fitting note for them to raise.
We hear the after-shout that rings
For them who smote the power of kings;
The swelling triumph all would share;
But who the dark defeat would dare,
And boldly meet the wrath and woe
That wait the unsuccessful blow?
It were an envied fate, we deem,
To live a land's recorded theme,
  When we are in the tomb.
We, too, might yield the joys of home,
And waves of winter darkness roam,
  And tread a shore of bloom,
Knew we those waves, through coming time,
Should roll our names to every clime;
Felt we that millions on that shore
Should stand, our memory to adore.

But no glad vision burst in light
Upon the pilgrims' aching sight;
Their hearts no proud hereafter swelled;
Deep shadows veiled the way they held;
The yell of vengeance was the trump of fame;
Their monument, a grave without a name.

Yet, strong in weakness, there they stand,
    On yonder ice-bound rock,
Stern and resolved, that faithful band,
    To meet fate's rudest shock.
Though anguish rends the father's breast,
For them, his dearest and his best,
    With him the waste who trod, —
Though tears that freeze the mother sheds
Upon her children's houseless heads, —
    The Christian turns to God!

In grateful adoration now,
Upon the barren sands they bow.
What tongue of joy e'er woke such prayer
As bursts in desolation there!
What arm of strength e'er wrought such power
As waits to crown that feeble hour!
    There into life an infant empire springs!

There falls the iron from the soul;
There Liberty's young accents roll
    Up to the King of kings!
To fair creation's farthest bound
That thrilling summons yet shall sound;
The dreaming nations shall awake,
And to their centre earth's old kingdoms shake.
Pontiff and prince, your sway
Must crumble from that day;
Before the loftier throne of Heaven
The hand is raised, the pledge is given,
One monarch to obey, one creed to own, —
That monarch, God, that creed, his word alone.

Spread out earth's holiest records here
Of days and deeds to reverence dear.
A zeal like this what pious legends tell!
    On kingdoms built
    In blood and guilt
The worshipers of vulgar triumph dwell;
  But what exploits with theirs shall page
    Who rose to bless their kind,
  Who left their nation and their age
    Man's spirit to unbind!
Who boundless seas passed o'er,

And boldly met, in every path,
Famine, and frost, and heathen wrath,
    To dedicate a shore
Where Piety's meek train might breathe their vow,
And seek their Maker with an unshamed brow;
Where Liberty's glad race might proudly come,
And set up there an everlasting home!

Oh, many a time it hath been told,
The story of those men of old:
For this fair Poetry hath wreathed
    Her sweetest, purest flower;
For this proud Eloquence hath breathed
    His strain of loftiest power:
Devotion, too, hath lingered round
Each spot of consecrated ground,
    And hill and valley blessed;
There, where our banished fathers strayed, —
There, where they loved, and wept, and prayed, —
There, where their ashes rest.

And never may they rest unsung
While Liberty can find a tongue.
Twine, Gratitude, a wreath for them,
More deathless than the diadem,

Who to life's noblest end,
   Gave up life's noblest powers,
And bade the legacy descend
   Down, down to us and ours.
CHARLES SPRAGUE.

HYMN.

FOR THE 22D OF DECEMBER, 1803.

When o'er the billows heaving deep
    The Fathers of our race,
The precepts of their God to keep,
    Sought here their resting-place,

That gracious God their path prepared,
    Preserved from every harm,
And still for their protection bared
    His everlasting arm.

His breath, inspiring every gale,
    Impels them o'er the main;
His guardian angel spreads the sail,
    And tempests howl in vain.

For them old ocean's rocks are smoothed;
    December's face grows mild;
To vernal airs her blasts are soothed,
    And all their rage beguiled.

HYMN.

When Famine rolls her haggard eyes,
   His ever bounteous hand
Abundance from the sea supplies,
   And treasure from the sand.

Nor yet his tender mercies cease,
   His overruling plan
Inclines to gentleness and peace
   The heart of savage man.

And can our stony bosoms be
   To all these wonders blind,
Nor swell with thankfulness to Thee,
   O Parent of mankind?

All gracious God, inflame our zeal;
   Dispense one blessing more:
Grant us thy boundless love to feel,
   Thy goodness to adore.

                   JOHN QUINCY ADAMS.

ODE.

Sons of New England sires!
Why do your altar-fires
    Flame up on high;
Why from your festal board
Wakes the loud anthem, poured
Joyous, with one accord,
    Winged for the sky?

Not for the voice that spoke
Triumph — when Britain's yoke
    Burst with your chains;
Not for the heroes brave,
Bleeding by Charles' wave,
Not for the patriot's grave,
    Wake ye your strains;

But for the Pilgrim-band,
They who from Leyden's land
    Dared the rough sea;

ODE.

Braving the ocean vast,
Scorning the wintry blast,
So they might find, at last,
    Room for the free.

Hark, how the thunder peals!
See, how the brave ship reels,
    Whirled in the brine!
Courage! the God that wears
Storm-robes, the good man spares:
Pilgrim! He hears your prayers, —
    Joy to your line!

Nobly the Mayflower bows
While the dark wave she ploughs
    On to the West;
Till from the tempest's shock
Proudly she lands her flock,
Where, on old Plymouth-rock,
    Freedom found rest.

Lo! from yon starry sphere
Spirits in light appear,
    Glorious, but few.
Pilgrims! we see you now;
Fathers! to you we bow;

Hear, then, your children's vow,
   Still to be true.

Join, brothers, heart and hand,
Sons of the Pilgrim-band!
   Swear now to be
All that your fathers sought,—
All that their virtue wrought,—
So shall your sons be taught
   How to be free!

RUFUS DAWES.

CLARK'S ISLAND.

Hail, hallowed spot! where Freedom's rays
First darted o'er the wanderer's ways,
  And gave him rest,
First brought the dawn of brighter days, —
  Thy shores are blest!

But dark the clouds that lingered round
The island which the Pilgrim found,
  In time long gone,
And deep and drear the thrilling sound
  Of gathering storm.

Aye, dark indeed, whose night of yore
That rocked the Mayflower near thy shore
  On wintry tides, —
For dark the waves that round thee roar,
  And wash thy sides.

But bright the star that lent its ray
To bear the traveler on his way
  From childhood's seat,

That lighted up so fair a day
    For his retreat.

Oh, who would ask a holier bed
Than where he laid his weary head,
    And nobly slept,
For though the Pilgrim long hath fled,
    His spirit's left.

Then hail the spot where first the sound
Of Freedom shook the sacred ground
    In early days,
And filled the hills and forests round
    With gladsome praise.

HERSEY B. GOODWIN.

HYMN.

O God, beneath thy guiding hand
   Our exiled fathers crossed the sea;
And when they trod the wintry strand
   With prayer and psalm they worshiped Thee.

Thou heard'st, well pleased, the song, the prayer:
   Thy blessing came; and still its power
Shall onward through all ages bear
   The memory of that holy hour.

Laws, freedom, truth, and faith in God
   Came with those exiles o'er the waves;
And where their pilgrim feet have trod
   The God they trusted guards their graves.

And here thy name, O God of love,
   Their children's children shall adore,
Till these eternal hills remove,
   And spring adorns the earth no more.

LEONARD BACON.

ODE.

Let children learn the mighty deeds
    Their sires achieved of old;
And still, as time to time succeeds,
    To them the tale unfold.

Here while we fondly trace the scene
    This joyous day recalls,
Let youth with reverend age convene
    Within these hallowed walls.

Their pious toils, their just rewards,
    Returning tributes claim,
While faithful history records
    Each venerable name.

Here first the temple's votive fane,
    Aspiring, sought the skies,
And here Religion's exiled train
    Bade sacred altars rise.

ODE.

No longer now the roaming hordes
    Unhallowed vigils keep;
No more affrighted mothers guard
    Their cradled infants' sleep:

But social arts and peaceful homes
    This favored land endear,
Where fields and masts and rising domes
    With scattered grace appear.

Let musing strangers view the ground,
    Here seek tradition's lore,
Where Pilgrims walked on holy ground
    With God in days of yore;

And where around the savage tribe
    Alarmed with horrid yells,
Assembling crowds secure imbibe
    What holy legend tells.

Let children emulate their deeds,
    Their choral praises sing;
So shall the muse, as time proceeds,
    Her meed of incense bring.

                SAMUEL DAVIS.

HYMN.

DECEMBER 22, 1806.

Our Fathers' God! to Thee we raise,
With one accord, the song of praise;
To Thee our grateful tribute pay
Oft as returns this festal day.

With tearful eyes we here will trace
Thy wonders to the Pilgrim race;
And while those wonders we explore,
Their names extol, thy name adore.

Our Fathers' God! Thy own decree
Ordained the Pilgrims to be free;
In foreign lands they owned thy care,
And found a safe asylum there.

When the wide main they traversed o'er,
And landed on this sea-beat shore,
The Pilgrims' Rock must e'er proclaim
Thy guardian care was still the same.

HYMN.

Our Fathers' God! while here we trace
Our lineage to the Pilgrim race,
Oh, may we like those Pilgrims live,
And in the sons the sires revive.

Our Fathers' God! to Thee we raise,
With one accord, the song of praise;
To Thee our grateful tribute pay
Oft as returns this festal day.

REV. DR. HOLMES.

FOREFATHERS' DAY.

DECEMBER 22.

The memory of the faithful dead
  Be on their children's hearts this day!
Your fathers' God, their host that led,
  Will shield you through the stormy way.

Your Saviour bids you seek and save
  The trampled and the oppressed of earth;
At his command the storm to brave,
  Faithful and true! come boldly forth!

Their suffering though your souls must share, —
  Though pride oppress and hate condemn, —
Stand up! and breathe your fearless prayer
  For those in bonds, as bound with them.

Unheeded fall the fierce command
  That bids the struggling soul be dumb!
Shout with a voice to rouse a land!
  Bid the free martyr spirit come!

Searcher of hearts, to Thee we bow, —
　Uphold us with thy staff and rod;
Our fervent hearts are ready now, —
　We come to do thy will, O God!

M. W. CHAPMAN.

SONG.

DECEMBER 22, 1807.

Hail! sons of the Pilgrims, assembled to pay
   Festivity's rite to our fathers in glory!
May the ardor of friendship enliven the lay,
   And their virtues be told, while we glow with
     the story.
       With the patriot's fire
       Be enflamed each desire,
To all that is noble each bosom aspire;
For, long as old earth on her axle shall turn,
On the altars of freemen pure incense should
   burn.

When tyranny bigotry's banners upreared,
   Those fathers, for conscience, for freedom, self-
   banished,
Confiding in Heaven, o'er the wild billow steered,
   And in Holland found refuge, while bigotry
   vanished:
       There, strangers awhile
       From their friends — from their Isle,

PILGRIM HALL, PLYMOUTH.

SONG. 57

See them sojourn in hope, — in adversity smile;
Till raising again the white sail to the wind,
They plough the rough main, their own region
  to find.

Long tossing in doubt, o'er the wildering wave,
  The pilot yet timid to brave the commotion;
Them hailing to freedom, from perils to save,
  Columbia displayed her blue skirt from the ocean.
    In Plymouth they land,
    On the bleak barren strand,
Yet they're strong in their shield — an omnipotent hand:
For there to their wanderings a period they find,
And their brows with the laurels of freedom first bind.

The savage his quiver exhausted in vain;
  He rose — but his tomahawk idle descended:
Independent, the Pilgrims moved free o'er the plain;
  Magnanimity nerved them — their bravery defended:
    Though environed by foes,
    They found calm repose,

While the wilderness blossomed and smiled like
   the rose :
Till late to the grave, as they smoothly declined,
To their offspring their virtue, a birthright, re-
   signed.

When Albion their heirs to enslave vainly strove,
   When lunatic Gallia committed aggression,
They lowered in the combat — the assailants hence
   drove,
   Independence they won — of their rights kept
      possession.
         Then oft will we tell,
         In the feast of the shell,
The deeds of their fame, till with transports we
   swell ;
And teach the sweet infant, that smiles on his
   sire,
To pant for like fame, and to glow with like fire.

Though society's base were by faction assailed,
   Or, the bane of our safety, by flattery were var-
      nished ;
Though the veteran be seen in his hamlet un-
   mailed —
   Retired from the Council, his laurels untar-
      nished :

	Yet the foe on our coast,
	Lo! he flies to his post;
His valor impels — in himself he's a host;
And with him the sons of New England shall fly,
Resolved to live honored, or nobly to die.

Yes, now from the East see aggression impend!
	Ye venerable shades, your remembrance shall fire us;
Our rights shall be sacred — our laws we'll defend;
	Our union shall strengthen — true glory inspire us:
		If the bolt be but hurled,
		Shall our flags be unfurled;
	Though *few*, yet their fame shall extend o'er the world;
	While the honors and laurels that deck our brave tars
	Shall end but with time, and but fade with the stars!

Thus, oft in our pilgrimage, memory shall glow,
	As the tale of the past comes with pleasure attendant;
And the boast of our nation, latest ages shall know, —

Our Fathers in Glory — their sons Independent!
    Then glad be your song
    Ye convivial throng;
Roll, roll the full chorus of rapture along:
For, long as old earth on her axle shall turn,
On the altars of freemen pure incense must burn.
            JOSEPH WARREN BRACKETT.

THE PILGRIM'S VISION.

In the hour of twilight shadows
   The Pilgrim sire looked out;
He thought of the "bloudy-Salvages"
   That lurked all round about,
Of Wituwamet's pictured knife
   And Pecksuot's whooping shout;
For the baby's limbs were feeble,
   Though his father's arms were stout.

His home was a freezing cabin,
   Too bare for the hungry rat;
Its roof was thatched with ragged grass,
   And bald enough of that.
The hole that served for casement
   Was glazed with an ancient hat;
And the ice was gently thawing
   From the log whereon he sat.

Along the dreary landscape
   His eyes went to and fro,

The trees all clad in icicles,
    The streams that did not flow ;
A sudden thought flashed o'er him, —
    A dream of long ago, —
He smote his leathern jerkin,
    And murmured, " Even so ! "

" Come hither, God-be-glorified,
    And sit upon my knee,
Behold the dream unfolding,
    Whereof I spake to thee
By the winter's hearth in Leyden,
    And on the stormy sea ;
True is the dream's beginning, —
    So may its ending be !

" I saw in the naked forest
    Our scattered remnant cast,
A screen of shivering branches
    Between them and the blast ;
The snow was falling round them,
    The dying fell as fast ;
I looked to see them perish,
    When lo ! the vision passed.

" Again mine eyes were opened : —
    The feeble had waxed strong,

The babes had grown to sturdy men,
  The remnant was a throng;
By shadowed lake and winding stream,
  And all the shores along.
The howling demons quaked to hear
  The Christian's godly song.

" They slept, — the village fathers, —
  By river, lake, and shore,
When far adown the steep of time
  The vision rose once more;
I saw along the winter snow
  A spectral column pour,
And, high above their broken ranks
  A tattered flag they bore.

" Their Leader rode before them,
  Of bearing calm and high,
The light of Heaven's own kindling
  Throned in his awful eye.
These were a Nation's champions,
  Her dread appeal to try;
God for the right! I faltered,
  And, lo! the train passed by.

" Once more, — the strife is ended,
  The solemn issue tried,

The Lord of Hosts, his mighty arm
  Has helped our Israel's side;
Gray stone and grassy hillock
  Told where the martyrs died,
But peaceful smiles the harvest,
  And stainless flows the tide.

" A crash, — as when some swollen cloud
  Cracks o'er the tangled trees!
With side to side, and spar to spar,
  Whose smoking decks are these?
I know St. George's blood-red cross,
  Thou Mistress of the Seas, —
But what is she, whose streaming bars
  Roll out before the breeze?

" Ah, well her iron ribs are knit,
  Whose thunders strive to quell
The bellowing throats, the blazing lips,
  That pealed the Armada's knell!
The mist was cleared — a wreath of stars
  Rose o'er the crimsoned swell,
And, wavering from its haughty peak,
  The cross of England fell!

" O trembling Faith! though dark the morn,
  A heavenly torch is thine;

While feebler races melt away,
　　And paler orbs decline,
Shall still the fiery pillar's ray
　　Along thy pathway shine,
To light the chosen tribe that sought
　　This Western Palestine!

"I see the living tide roll on;
　　It crowns with flaming towers
The icy cape of Labrador,
　　The Spaniard's 'land of flowers!'
It streams beyond the splintered ridge
　　That parts the northern shores;
From eastern rock to sunset wave
　　The Continent is ours!"

He ceased, — the grim old soldier-saint, —
　　Then softly bent to cheer
The pilgrim-child, whose wasting face
　　Was meekly turned to hear;
And drew his toil-worn sleeve across,
　　To brush the manly tear
From cheeks that never changed in woe,
　　And never blanched in fear.

The weary pilgrim slumbers,
   His resting-place unknown;
His hands were crossed, his lids were closed,
   The dust was o'er him strown;
The drifting soil, the mouldering leaf,
   Along the sod were blown;
His mound has melted into earth,
   His memory lives alone.

So let it live unfading,
   The memory of the dead,
Long as the pale anemone
   Springs where their tears were shed,
Or, raining in the summer's wind
   In flakes of burning red,
The wild rose sprinkles with its leaves
   The turf where once they bled!

Yea, when the frowning bulwarks
   That guard this holy strand
Have sunk beneath the trampling surge
   In beds of sparkling sand,
While in the waste of ocean
   One hoary rock shall stand,
Be this its latest legend, —
   Here was the Pilgrims' land!

                      O. W. HOLMES.

HYMN.

Sons of the noble sires
Who braved proud ocean's waves
   For freedom's sake!
Say — will ye quench those fires
Their faith and love inspires;
And, standing on their graves,
   Their paths forsake?

Shall freedom find a grave,
On this blood-ransomed soil?
   Must we be *slaves?*
Our fleeting lives to save,
Must we no mercy crave,
But with the bondman toil,
   Branded as knaves?

Shall despots *here* bear sway, —
The iron sceptre *here* display,
   Our lips to close?
Sons of the Pilgrims! say —
Will ye these lords obey,

And ask them when you may
　　The truth disclose ?

No — *no!*　We answer, *no!*
The truth we 'll fearless show
　　While breath remains ;
Did not our Saviour so ?
Would He the truth forego ?
Or shrink when bade the foe,
　　T" scape from pains ?

While then a slave is found,
While man by man is bound,
　　We 'll speak and pray ;
We 'll wear the bondman's chains,
We 'll bear the bondman's pains,
We 'll hear when he complains, —
　　We 'll do and say.

GEORGE RUSSELL.

THE LANDING OF THE PILGRIM FATHERS IN NEW ENGLAND.

The breaking waves dashed high
   On a stern and rock-bound coast,
And the woods against a stormy sky
   Their giant branches tossed;

And the heavy night hung dark
   The hills and waters o'er,
When a band of exiles moored their bark
   On the wild New England shore.

Not as the conqueror comes,
   They, the true-hearted, came;
Not with the roll of the stirring drums,
   And the trumpet that sings of fame:

Not as the flying come,
   In silence and in fear;
They shook the depths of the desert gloom
   With their hymns of lofty cheer.

Amidst the storm they sang,
    And the stars heard, and the sea:
And the sounding aisles of the dim woods rang
    To the anthem of the free!

The ocean eagle soared
    From his nest by the white wave's foam:
And the rocking pines of the forest roared, —
    This was their welcome home!

There were men with hoary hair
    Amidst that pilgrim band;
Why had *they* come to wither there,
    Away from their childhood's land?

There was woman's fearless eye,
    Lit by her deep love's truth;
There was manhood's brow serenely high,
    And the fiery heart of youth.

What sought they thus afar?
    Bright jewels of the mine?
The wealth of seas, the spoils of war? —
    They sought a faith's pure shrine!

Ay, call it holy ground,
  The soil where first they trod:
They have left unstained what there they found,—
  Freedom to worship God.

Mrs. Hemans.

THE PILGRIM FATHERS.

A voice of grief and anger,
    Of pity mixed with scorn,
Moans o'er the waters of the West,
    Through fire and darkness borne;
And fiercer voices join it, —
    A wild, triumphant yell!
For England's foes, on ocean slain,
    Have heard it where they fell.

What is that voice which cometh
    Athwart the spectred sea?
The voice of men who left their homes
    To make their children free;
Of men whose hearts were torches
    For Freedom's quenchless fire;
Of men whose mothers brave brought forth
    The sire of Franklin's sire.

They speak! the Pilgrim Fathers
    Speak to you from their graves!

For earth hath muttered to their bones
   That we are soulless slaves!
The Bradfords, Carvers, Winslows,
   Have heard the worm complain
That less than men oppress the men
   Whose sires were Pym and Vane!

What saith the voice which boometh
   Athwart the upbraiding waves?
"Though slaves are ye, our sons are free;
   Then why will you be slaves?
The children of your fathers
   Were Hampden, Pym, and Vane!"
Land of the sires of Washington,
   Bring forth such men again!

EBENEZER ELLIOTT,
the " Corn-Law Rhymer " of England.

TWO HUNDRED YEARS AGO.

SUNG AT THE PUBLIC DINNER AT PLYMOUTH, DECEMBER 22, 1820.

Come, listen to my story,
   Though often told before,
Of men who passed to glory,
   Through toil and travail sore;
Of men who did for conscience' sake
   Their native land forego,
And sought a home and freedom here,
   Two hundred years ago.

Oh, 't was no earth-born passion
   That bade the adventurers stray;
The world and all its fashion
   With them had passed away.
A voice from Heaven bade them look
   Above the things below,
When here they sought a resting-place,
   Two hundred years ago.

Oh, dark the scene and dreary,
  When here they set them down;
Of storms and billows weary,
  And chilled with winter's frown.
Deep moaned the forests to the wind,
  Loud howled the savage foe,
While here their evening prayer arose,
  Two hundred years ago.

'T would drown the heart in sorrow
  To tell of all their woes;
No respite could they borrow,
  But from the grave's repose.
Yet naught could daunt the Pilgrim Band,
  Or sink their courage low,
Who came to plant the Gospel here,
  Two hundred years ago.

With humble prayer and fasting,
  In every strait and grief,
They sought the Everlasting,
  And found a sure relief.
Their cov'nant God o'ershadowed them,
  Their shield from every foe,
And gave them here a dwelling-place,
  Two hundred years ago.

Of fair New England's glory
   They laid the corner-stone ;
This praise in deathless story
   Their grateful sons shall own.
Prophetic, they foresaw in time
   A mighty state should grow,
For them, a few faint Pilgrims here,
   Two hundred years ago.

If greatness be in daring,
   Our Pilgrim Sires were great,
Whose sojourn here, unsparing,
   Disease and famine wait ;
And oft their treacherous foes combined
   To lay the strangers low,
While founding here their commonwealth.
   Two hundred years ago.

Though seeming over zealous
   In things by us deemed light,
They were but duly jealous
   Of power usurping right.
They nobly chose to part with all
   Most dear to men below,
To worship here their God in peace,
   Two hundred years ago.

From seeds they sowed with weeping
    Our richest harvests rise;
We still the fruits are reaping
    Of Pilgrim enterprise.
Then, grateful, we to them will pay
    The debt of fame we owe,
Who planted here the tree of life,
    Two hundred years ago.

As comes this period yearly,
    Around our cheerful fires
We 'll think and tell how dearly
    Our comforts cost our sires;
For them will wake the votive song,
    And bid the canvas glow,
Who fixed the home of freedom here,
    Two hundred years ago.

JAMES FLINT.

HYMN.

SUNG AT THE CELEBRATION OF 1824.

Holy spot, where glowing choirs
Oft have wakened grateful lyres,
Oft have kindled grateful fires,
    O'er the Pilgrim's grave!

Once again we press the shore,
Where our Fathers sternly swore
Ocean should forget to roar
    Ere they would be slaves.

Hail the dawn when Freedom's rays
Hushed Columbia's icy face;
Sweeter strains arise of praise
    Than from Memnon's harp.

Hail the spot, our Sires' retreat;
Hail the waves that round them beat;
Hail the Rock that bore their feet,
    When their wanderings ceased!

Fancy paints in yonder bay
The bark that broke the Pilgrim's way ;
The *Cradle* where our nation lay
    In her infant days.

See the boat approach the land,
Freighted with the pious band ;
See, they kneel upon the strand,
    Warm with gratitude.

Vent your fury, wind and flood,
Freedom's bark is safely moored ;
Freedom's sons, with hearts assured,
    Now their work begin.

Gloomy scenes await the brave,
Savage foes around them rave ;
Carver fills an early grave,
    Hope well-nigh expires.

But to Faith's reluming eye
Visions bright in prospect lie ;
E'en a triumph 't were to die,
    If in conscience free.

Still above the sacred dead
Future crowds shall yearly tread ;

>   Blooming youth and hoary head,
>   Meet around their urns.
>
> Oft shall Genius' fluent tongue
> Trace the story, swell the song;
> Oft amidst the listening throng
>   Thrill the feeling soul.
>
> Ye who 've sprung from noble blood,
> Men who spurned the tyrant's rod,
> Men who bowed to none but God,
>   Here your vows repeat:
>
> "By their pious shades we swear,
> By their toils and perils here,
> We will guard with jealous care
>   Law and Liberty."

WILLIAM P. LUNT.

ODE.

Not all the loftiest memories
    That rose on earlier days,
When, with the trump and sacrifice,
    And swelling pomp of praise,
Men gathered to their pillared halls,
    'Mid garlands, joy, and wine,
To gaze on heroes round the walls,
    In marble made divine,

And pour the deep libation there
    To victors passed away;
Or minds whose wonders, rich and rare,
    Poured splendor on their day, —
Not all in finer hearts can vie
    With those that summon here,
To lift, on Freedom's clarion high,
    The anthem of our cheer!

We sing a nobler race than passed
    In ancient times to glory:

We sing of deeds that shall outlast,
    In fame, all classic story;
Of men who fought for God, and gave
    Home for a desert shore, —
With hearts too panoplied and brave
    To quail beneath its roar!

Of *Exiles* of a deathless line,
    And proud, unshrinking brow;
Lone *Pilgrims* to a rocky shrine,
    Where a people bend them now:
A rocky shrine, unsheltered, rude,
    Where the wild wolf from his lair
Shrieked through the pathless solitude,
    And broke the voice of prayer!

We sing of heroes who outdid
    The boast of chivalry:
Whose valor braved the shock amid
    A stormy sea and sky;
Whose deeds were deeds of mercy, done
    To persecuted man;
Whose wreaths were wreaths of triumph, wo
    In *Virtue's* fearless van!

New England's Fathers! — men who dared
    The agony of years;

Whom pale *Oppression* never spared,
    But could not bow to tears;
Who 'mid the howl of winter fled,
    And your banner here unfurled,
And *Conscience* in her pride outled
    Unfettered to the world!

Pilgrims of glory! there shall rise
    Fast praise from heart and tongue
Of all for whom in sacrifice,
    Like martyr-saints, ye sprung;
And their children's children shall outpour,
    From echoing clime to clime,
New pæans for the toils ye bore
    In a nation's morning-time.

Two hundred years their cloudy wings
    Expand above your graves;
And lo, what wide-flashed glory flings
    O'er all New England's waves!
Fathers of Liberty! to ye
    We lift the wine-cup now;
Yours be the hallowed memory
    That consecrates our vow.

And should the voice of prophecy
    That 's doomed us to the dust

E'er chant the requiem of the *Free*,
 By tyranny accursed,
Oh, be a remnant true to her!
 Sons whom *New England* bore,
Together seek one sepulchre
 On *Plymouth's* sounding shore!

GRENVILLE MELLEN.

HYMN.

WRITTEN FOR DECEMBER 22, 1831.

The brittle bark is on the gale,
Heaven guides her course, and swells the sail;
The Pilgrims reach yon welcome shore,
All vocal with the songs they pour.

Keen round them blows the winter's air;
The weary wanderers kneel for prayer;
From opening clouds a voice is given:
Pilgrims, there's "nothing true but heaven"!

What though no mystic cloud, nor flame,
Led on the wanderers as they came?
By faith they saw the one true God
Was guardian of the way they trod.

God of our fathers, hear our prayer!
This church be still and long thy care;
And grateful at this day's return
Fresh incense at thy shrine shall burn.

How long shall erring mortals feel
The exclusive, the unholy zeal
The golden gates of heaven to close
On all they dare to call thy foes?

These doors we open fling, and free
To all, great God, who call on Thee;
If warm their hearts in Christian deeds,
Who shall exclude them for their creeds?

Here may they drink from living springs
The light and life the gospel brings;
And, healed by Siloa's waters, deem
Thy power and bounty feed the stream.

Rise, Bethlehem's star, and spread thy blaze
To every land in cheering rays,
Till angels, in the glad employ,
Cast down their crowns and shout for joy.

ANONYMOUS.

NATIONAL HYMN.

God hath from age to age
Raised hero up, and sage,
    For Liberty;
He bared the Red Sea's sand,
He led to Plymouth's strand,
And planted in this Western land
    The Fathers free.

Eternal, low we bow!
This land invokes Thee now,
    The children hear!
May wrong and outrage cease,
Wisdom and worth increase;
Be justice, truth, and faith, and peace
    Than gold more dear.

Aught friendly to our race
Quicken our souls to embrace
    With will right good.
May we, great God, in Thee,

One common Father see;
In man one great fraternity,
    Made of one blood!

Us, Father, Thou hast given
The highest under Heaven
    To rise or fall.
Let this Republic shine
With rising light benign,
And thus fulfill the grand design,
    The good of all.

DAVID LEE CHILD.

REMEMBRANCE OF THE PILGRIMS.

   With joy I heard them say,
     When roving far abroad,
 On this, their landing day,
    We 'll praise the Pilgrims' God.
      I knew the cry,
        I 'll join the song;
       Thy courts we 'll throng,
     O Thou Most High!

   This day let all awake,
    And sing the mighty dead,
 Who first, for Zion's sake,
    O'er raging oceans fled.
      Had not our God
        Preserved that flock,
       Safe on the rock
     They ne'er had trod.

   At once their temples rose;
    Our schools were founded then;

Nor could their mightier foes
  Withstand those valiant men.
But vain their skill,
  And vain their sword,
Had not the Lord
Upheld them still.

Peace to that holy ground,
  That consecrated spot,
The first our fathers found
  Where tyrants trouble not!
We'll sound abroad,
  Where'er we roam,
The Pilgrims' home,
The Pilgrims' God!

ANONYMOUS.

HYMN.

Lo, the rising star of Freedom
    Once our Pilgrim Fathers blest;
By her light ordained to lead them
    To the land of promised rest.
        Star of heaven!
        Star of heaven!
    Traveling toward the distant west.

While their countless toils enduring,
    Faith the promise kept in sight:
For themselves and sons securing
    Home and country, truth and light.
        Star of heaven!
        Star of heaven!
    Pointing to Jehovah's might.

Now the relics round us lying,
    Grateful children guard their clay;
While their spirits, never dying,
    Hope has borne on wings away.

Star of heaven!
Star of heaven!
Guiding to a brighter day.

Raise we honors to their merit,
    Temples sculptured with their name?
No! their virtues to inherit
    Seals their bright and conscious fame.
        Star of heaven!
        Star of heaven!
High they shine with ceaseless flame.

See the lights around us gleaming,
    Still to guide the Pilgrims' eyes:
See the star of empire, beaming,
    Bids their children's glory rise.
        Star of heaven!
        Star of heaven!
Glowing still in western skies.

S. DEANE.

THE SAINTED SIRES.

While Pilgrims' sons, a festive throng,
   To sainted sires their homage pay,
Be this the burthen, the burthen of their song,
   And rapture animate the lay:

CHORUS.

    Hail, ye Pilgrims!
   Ye sainted Pilgrims, hail!
Till hours, and years, and time shall fail.

By heroes led, by virtue warmed,
   Conducted by the Almighty hand,
They braved the ocean, the ocean and the storm,
   And freedom sought in unknown land.

The perils of the ocean past,
   Fresh dangers quickly them surround;
Shrill screams the savage — the savage o'er the blast,
   And rocks and hills repeat the sound.

The barbarous foe to battle fly,
  Intent on bloody deeds and spoil;
Swift flies the arrow, the arrow through the sky,
  But victory crowns the Pilgrim's toil.

Success attend the good and brave,
  The meed of praise to them belongs;
Virtue shall triumph — shall triumph o'er the grave,
  And angels join their rapturous songs.

Hail ye Pilgrims!
Ye sainted Pilgrims, hail!
When earth, and sky, and time shall fail.

ANONYMOUS.

ODE.

FOR THE CELEBRATION AT PLYMOUTH, DECEMBER 22, 1824.

The Pilgrim Fathers, — where are they?
   The waves that brought them o'er
Still roll in the bay, and throw their spray,
   As they break along the shore;
Still roll in the bay, as they rolled that day
   When the Mayflower moored below,
When the sea around was black with storms,
   And white the shore with snow.

The mists that wrapped the Pilgrim's sleep
   Still brood upon the tide;
And his rocks yet keep their watch by the deep,
   To stay its waves of pride.
But the snow-white sail that he gave to the gale,
   When the heavens looked dark, is gone;
As an angel's wing, through an opening cloud,
   Is seen, and then withdrawn.

The Pilgrim exile, — sainted name!
   The hill whose icy brow

Rejoiced, when he came, in the morning's flame,
  In the morning's flame burns now;
And the moon's cold light, as it lay that night
  On the hill-side and the sea,
Still lies where he laid his houseless head;
  But the Pilgrim, — where is he?

The Pilgrim Fathers are at rest;
  When summer's throned on high,
And the world's warm breast is in verdure dressed,
  Go, stand on the hill where they lie.
The earliest ray of the golden day
  On that hallowed spot is cast;
And the evening sun, as he leaves the world,
  Looks kindly on that spot last.

The Pilgrim *spirit* has not fled:
  It walks in noon's broad light;
And it watches the bed of the glorious dead,
  With the holy stars, by night.
It watches the bed of the brave who have bled,
  And shall guard this ice-bound shore
Till the waves of the bay, where the Mayflower lay,
  Shall foam and freeze no more.

JOHN PIERPONT.

HYMN FOR DECEMBER 22, 1870.

Great God of all, in humble, grateful prayer,
   We come before Thee now on bended knee,
To thank Thee that Thou didst our fathers spare
   From the wild dangers of a wintry sea.

We thank Thee that when dangers greater far
   Encompassed them, that brave hearts might appall,
Thou didst support them, and didst let the Star
   Of Hope shine on their hearts, and strengthen all.

And we their children, on this joyous day,
   No longer peril-driven or tempest-tossed,
Approach thy throne in thankfulness, and pray
   Our fathers' bright example be not lost.

May we like them have strength and courage given,
   Bear bravely up, e'en tho' we feel the rod;
Know that a life well spent leads on to Heaven,
   And duty's paths are but the paths to God.

                        NATHANIEL SPOONER.

STANZAS FROM "THE PRESENT CRISIS."

'T is as easy to be heroes as to sit the idle slaves
Of a legendary virtue carved upon our fathers'
    graves;
Worshipers of light ancestral make the present
    light a crime;
Was the Mayflower launched by cowards, steered
    by men behind their time?
Turn those tracks toward Past or Future that
    make Plymouth Rock sublime?

They were men of present valor, stalwart old icono-
    clasts,
Unconvinced by axe or gibbet that all virtue was
    the Past's;
But we make their truth our falsehood, thinking
    that hath made us free,
Hoarding it in mouldy parchments, while our ten-
    der spirits flee
The rude grasp of that great Impulse which drove
    them across the sea.

They have rights who dare maintain them; we are traitors to our sires,
Smothering in their holy ashes Freedom's new-lit altar fires.
Shall we make their creed our jailer? Shall we, in our haste to slay,
From the tombs of the old prophets steal the funeral lamps away,
To light up the martyr-fagots round the prophets of to-day?

New occasions teach new duties; time makes ancient good uncouth;
They must upward still, and onward, who would keep abreast of truth.
Lo, before us gleam her camp-fires! We ourselves must Pilgrims be;
Launch our Mayflower, and steer boldly through the desperate winter sea,
Nor attempt the Future's portal with the Past's blood-rusted key.

J. R. LOWELL.

December, 1845.

www.ingramcontent.com/pod-product-compliance
Lightning Source LLC
Chambersburg PA
CBHW030410170426
43202CB00010B/1562